D0241754

LET'S EXPLORE BRITAIN

Coasts

JAMES NIXON

a Capstone company — publishers for children

Raintree is an imprint of Capstone Global Library Limited, a company incorporated in England and Wales having its registered office at 264 Banbury Road, Oxford, OX2 7DY – Registered company number: 6695582

www.raintree.co.uk
myorders@raintree.co.uk

Text © Capstone Global Library Limited 2018
The moral rights of the proprietor have been asserted.

All rights reserved. No part of this publication may be reproduced in any form or by any means (including photocopying or storing it in any medium by electronic means and whether or not transiently or incidentally to some other use of this publication) without the written permission of the copyright owner, except in accordance with the provisions of the Copyright, Designs and Patents Act 1988 or under the terms of a licence issued by the Copyright Licensing Agency, Saffron House, 6–10 Kirby Street, London EC1N 8TS (www.cla.co.uk). Applications for the copyright owner's written permission should be addressed to the publisher.

Edited by James Nixon
Designed by Keith Williams, sprout.uk.com
Picture Research by James Nixon
Production by Discovery Books
Originated by Capstone Global Library Limited
Printed and bound in China

ISBN 978 1 4747 5899 4
22 21 20 19 18
10 9 8 7 6 5 4 3 2 1

Coventry City Council	
CEN*	
3 8002 02381 501 4	
Askews & Holts	May-2018
J551.457094 JUNIOR N	£12.99

British Library Cataloguing in Publication Data
A full catalogue record for this book is available from the British Library.

Acknowledgements
We would like to thank the following for permission to reproduce photographs:
Cover Image (Ulmus Media/Shutterstock); Alamy: pp. 4 (parkerphotography), 11 (A.P.S. UK), 12 (B.O'Kane), 16 (Premaphotos), 18 (Andrew Ray), 22 (Ashley Cooper pics), 25 (gkphotography); Shutterstock: pp. 5 (Marten_House), 6 (Ian Woolcock), 7 (Philip Hector), 8 (Hadrian), 9 (Billy Stock), 10 (Doug Armand), 13 (Iain McGillivray), 14 (Ian Dyball), 15 (Francesco de Marco), 17 (Andrew Paul Deer), 19 (Tony Mills), 20 (Wim Claes), 21 (Phonix_a Pk.sarote), 23 (Pefkos), 24 (skyearth), 26 (DJTaylor), 27 (Shaun Wilkinson), 28 (Martin Lisner), 29 (Jen Burrows).

We would like to thank Dr Gillian Fyfe for her invaluable help in the preparation of this book.

Every effort has been made to contact copyright holders of material reproduced in this book. Any omissions will be rectified in subsequent printings if notice is given to the publisher.

All the internet addresses (URLs) given in this book were valid at the time of going to press. However, due to the dynamic nature of the internet, some addresses may have changed, or sites may have changed or ceased to exist since publication. While the author and publisher regret any inconvenience this may cause readers, no responsibility for any such changes can be accepted by either the author or the publisher.

Contents

What is a coast?

The coast is the edge of the land next to the sea. Some areas of the coastline are rocky, with tall **cliffs**. Other parts are flat, sandy or muddy. Coasts are important places for people and wildlife.

Flocks of seagulls can be seen at many of Britain's beaches.

Ramsgate, Kent

Britain is a large island. Its coastline is huge and jagged. In total, the coastline measures over 11,000 miles (17,700 kilometres) in length. Many smaller islands surround Britain. Each of these have their own coastline. There are over 100 islands in the Hebrides in north-west Scotland alone.

A lighthouse sits at the tip of Neist Point on the Isle of Skye. Skye is one of the largest islands in the Hebrides.

Shaping the coast

The shape of Britain's coastline is created by the sea. Waves crash into the land. They break and wear rock down. This battle between the land and sea has lasted for millions of years. During storms, great winds blow across the sea. The winds can whip up giant waves.

Waves crash into a **headland** near Land's End in Cornwall.

Soft rock is worn away by waves more quickly than hard rock. Where the rock is soft, the sea can scoop out curved shapes in the coastline. These are called **bays**. The sea leaves areas of harder rock jutting out into the sea. These are called **headlands**.

A small, sheltered bay is called a cove.

Lulworth Cove, Dorset

Cliffs and caves

On many parts of the coast, towering **cliffs** drop down to the sea. The rock in the cliffs is very slowly worn away by the sea. Waves make long holes called notches along the bottom of cliffs. Notches can cause chunks of rock and cliff to collapse into the sea.

These cliffs in East Sussex are made from chalk. They are called the Seven Sisters.

Pounding waves force water into cracks in cliffs. The cracks burst apart and this creates caves. At **headlands**, the sea can break all the way through caves to form **arches**. Arches eventually collapse. This leaves tall **stacks** of rock behind. Stacks can also fall down over time and become low **stumps**.

This arch on the Pembrokeshire coast is called the Green Bridge of Wales.

Stack

Building beaches

Beaches are formed by waves. The waves carry rock, stones, sand and shells onto the shore. Sandy beaches are made from very fine grains of rock and broken shells. You will often see sandy beaches in **bays**, where there is shelter and the water is calm. Small pebbles called **shingle** can also cover beaches.

Sandy beaches such as Kynance Cove in Cornwall are popular with **tourists**.

The strength of waves can move beaches along a coastline. The angle of waves can sometimes push beaches out into the sea. A long stretch of sand or shingle sticking out from the land is called a **spit**. Spits will curve where the direction of the wind and waves changes.

Spit

A spit over 5 kilometres (3 miles) long formed at Spurn Head, in East Yorkshire.

What is an estuary?

An estuary is the point where a river flows out and meets the sea. Estuaries can be narrow or many kilometres wide. Rivers slow down as they meet the sea. As they slow, tiny **particles** sink to the bottom of the river. These particles can build up to form enormous **mudflats**.

The estuary at Warrenpoint separates Northern Ireland from the Republic of Ireland.

Twice a day, the water level along the coast rises and falls. These are the **tides**. Mudflats and beaches are uncovered when the tide is low. At high tide, the sea pushes up estuaries and covers the mud. Seawater is salty. Rivers at estuaries are a mix of fresh and salty water.

The Thames Estuary, east of London, is very wide. The Thames Barrier is used to protect the city from high tides and stormy seas.

Wildlife on coasts

You can find lots of wildlife at coasts, such as seals, otters and birds. Animals feed on the fish in the sea. Large seals will crawl onto rocks and beaches to sunbathe. Mother seals give birth to their pups on the seashore.

Hundreds of seals breed on Horsey Beach in Norfolk every winter.

Noisy seabirds, such as gulls, gannets and razorbills, nest on steep **cliffs**. They keep their eggs safe on narrow, rocky ledges. Puffins nest in burrows on clifftops. Seabirds have special beaks to stop wriggly fish slipping out. The puffin can catch and hang on to ten fish at a time.

Many thousands of puffins live on the Farne Islands off the Northumberland coast. People can take boat trips to the islands to view the birds.

On rocky shores, pools of water are left behind when the tide goes out. Look inside these **rock pools** and you will find plenty of wildlife. Tiny fish, shrimps, crabs, **shellfish** and starfish live here. Seaweeds and anenomes are also found in rock pools. Anemones are bright, jelly-like creatures with waving **tentacles**.

Anemones, such as this dahlia anemone, look like flowers.

Powerful waves crash into the rocks every day. Many plants and animals need a strong grip to survive these waves. Seaweeds have **holdfasts** like roots that hold tight to the ground. Creatures, such as barnacles and mussels, have tough shells and cling to rocks. Limpets have a single super-strong foot that clamps down hard on the rock.

Limpets move slowly over rock, scraping off plant growth for food.

Dunes and mudflats

On sandy shores, the wind blows grains of sand up the beach. The sand can form ridges and hilly mounds called **dunes**. Tough grasses grow in the dunes and prevent them from being washed away. Sand lizards and snakes called adders sometimes live on the dunes' warm, sunny banks.

Sandwood Bay in Scotland is one of Britain's most beautiful beaches. Strong winds have created dunes at the back of the beach.

Mudflats look lifeless. But under the mud lives a huge variety of worms, shrimp and shellfish. These creatures attract **wading birds** looking for food. The wading birds fly onto the mudflats at low tides. Waders usually have long legs and long, pointed bills. They **probe** deep into the mud with their bills to feed.

These wading birds are called bar-tailed godwits.

Problems on the coast

Wildlife living in coastal areas face many threats. Storms and rising seas can wipe out precious **habitats** for ever. Humans pump millions of tons of **waste** into the seas every day. Dirty water can **poison** plants and animals. If oil spills from a ship into the sea it can cause great damage.

This razorbill has oil stuck in its feathers. A bird with damaged wings can die.

All kinds of rubbish washes up on beaches. Plastic does not rot away. It is very dangerous. Animals can swallow plastic or get trapped in bags or nets. In summer, beaches get very crowded. **Tourists** may drop litter. They can also frighten or disturb creatures on the shore.

If you visit the beach, never drop litter or leave rubbish behind.

In some places, the sea is wearing the coast away. People who live there are at risk of losing their homes. On the East Yorkshire coast, around 2 metres of soft **cliff** are worn away every year. Houses that were once inland are now perched on the clifftops. Many villages have ended up as rubble in the sea.

This road in the village of Skipsea, East Yorkshire, has almost vanished.

Even large cities are under threat from the sea. Walls are built on parts of the coast to block the waves. In some places, massive boulders are piled up on the beach. Beaches slow waves down. Fences called **groynes** are built on beaches. These stop sand being washed away by the sea.

The seaside **resort** of Blackpool is protected by a sea wall.

Sea wall

Cities and ports

Many cities in Britain were built along the coastline. Here, ships could arrive or leave, carrying goods or people. Towns and cities on the coast are called **ports**. Some ports, such as Glasgow and Belfast, became centres of the shipbuilding industry. Others, such as Plymouth and Portsmouth, grew as bases for the **Royal Navy**.

Portsmouth is now one of the busiest ports in Britain.

Factories are often built on the coast too. Ships can carry the **raw materials** that factories need, such as metals. When there are lots of factories and plenty of jobs, ports grow even bigger. Gigantic ships called supertankers transport oil to **refineries** and gas to **power stations**.

A huge ship heads out to sea from the port of Glasgow. It is carrying **cargo**.

Working on the coast

People have lived and worked on the coast for centuries. Fishermen have always hunted and gathered food from the sea. Many towns and villages still have fishing **harbours**. Fishing workers set out on boats to catch fish, crabs, lobsters and even octopus.

Fishing boats in the small harbour in Polperro, Cornwall.

Trawlers are fishing boats. They drag large nets through the sea. These nets can catch huge numbers of fish. Some ports developed large fishing industries. In the 1950s, Grimsby had the largest fishing **fleet** in the world. In Grimsby today, there are far fewer trawlers than in the past.

Out at sea, there are also jobs for people who look after **wind turbines.**

Trawler

Lots of people who live on the coast work in the **tourist** industry. This means that they provide services to people on holiday. Seaside towns became very popular in **Victorian** times. At **resorts** such as Brighton, hotels, **piers** and fairground rides were built. Brighton's amusements are just as popular today.

Fairground rides, such as this ferris wheel, are set up next to Brighton Beach.

The seaside is a great place to have fun or relax. You can play cricket on the beach, fly a kite or build sandcastles. In the sea, people can swim, surf or even zoom off on a **jet ski**. There are jobs for people at caravan sites, hotels and restaurants. Ice-cream sellers visit popular beaches in their vans.

Holidaymakers relax and play on Saundersfoot Beach, in south Wales.

Map of the UK

Here are the locations on the coast mentioned in this book.

Sandwood Bay

Neist Point

Glasgow

Farne Islands

Belfast

Warrenpoint

Blackpool

Skipsea

Grimsby • Spurn Head

Horsey

Saundersfoot

Green Bridge of Wales

Thames Estuary

London

Ramsgate

Brighton

Seven Sisters

Polperro

Portsmouth

Kynance Cove

Plymouth

Lulworth Cove

Land's End

Glossary

arch hole in a headland shaped like an arch

bay part of a coast where the land curves inwards

cargo goods carried on a ship, truck or aircraft

cliff steep rock face at the edge of the sea

dunes hills of sand near the sea

fleet group of ships

groyne wall or fence built on the seashore to stop a beach from being washed away

habitat home for an animal

harbour place on the coast where boats can be left safely

headland piece of land sticking out into the sea

holdfast stalk on a seaweed that grips tightly to the surface of rocks or the ground

jet ski small machine that can travel fast across the surface of the sea

mudflat area of low, muddy land near an estuary

particle very small piece or amount of something

pier long platform leading out to sea, which is used as a place for entertainments

poison substance that can harm or kill animals

port town or city where ships can load or unload

power station place where electrical power is produced

probe search

raw materials materials from which products are made

refinery factory where a substance, such as oil, has unwanted parts removed from it

resort place where many people stay on holiday

rock pool small pool among rocks on the seashore

Royal Navy military sea force of the UK, which includes warships

shellfish creatures that live in the sea and have shells

shingle small rounded pebbles on the seashore

spit long, narrow beach stretching out into the sea

stack tall pillar of rock standing in the sea

stump part of a sea stack that is left behind when the rest falls down

tentacles long, thin parts used for feeling and moving

tide regular change of the level of the sea on the shore

tourists people who travel for fun

Victorian relating to the time of Queen Victoria (1837–1901)

wading birds long-legged birds that walk in water or mud to feed

waste unwanted material that may be poisonous

wind turbines tall structures which convert wind energy into electricity

Find out more

Index

Books

British Seashore (Nature Detective), Victoria Munson (Wayland, 2016)

Coasts (Geography Corner), Ruth Thomson (Wayland, 2013)

Coasts (Mapping Britain's Landscape), Barbara Taylor (Franklin Watts, 2012)

Websites

www.bbc.co.uk/
schools/gcsebitesize/
geography/coasts/
Coastal Processes: *Find out how coasts are shaped by the sea.*

www.educationquizzes.
com/ks2/geography/
coasts/
Coast Quiz: *Test your knowledge of coastal features.*